Keyboard from the Beginning

by Christopher Hussey

Published by
Chester Music Limited
14-15 Berners Street, London W1T 3LJ, UK.

Exclusive Distributors:
Hal Leonard
7777 West Bluemound Road, Milwaukee, WI 53213
Email: info@halleonard.com
Hal Leonard Europe Limited
42 Wigmore Street Maryleborne, London, WIU 2 RN
Email: info@halleonardeurope.com
Hal Leonard Australia Pty. Ltd.
4 Lentara Court Cheltenham, Victoria, 9132 Australia
Email: info@halleonard.com.au

The author and publisher would like to thank Martha Cowan, our keyboard
player model, and Toby Knowles for his lyrics to 'Max The Monster'.

Illustrations by Ben Whitehouse
Diagrams by Richard Lemon at Fresh Lemon
Music processing and layout by Christopher Hussey
Edited by Toby Knowles

www.halleonard.com

Note for teachers

This introduction to playing the keyboard requires no previous experience of playing an instrument or of reading music. Beginning at the very start, students will be playing tunes and making music from their first lesson. It is equally appropriate for learning the keyboard or piano, and for individual or class teaching.

This teaching scheme is ideal for 6–12-year-olds, and through a selection of exciting original songs and well-loved favourites, it provides everything students will need to learn how to play. They begin by playing with their right hand only, and are then introduced to left-hand playing before they reach the stage where they are playing with both hands together. They will encounter many different musical styles and techniques, and learn about chords and other forms of accompaniment. There are also ideas for class activities, ensemble playing, musical games and composing.

Most of the tunes include lyrics to help with their rhythm — saying these lyrics aloud or singing them before playing will help students learn the tunes and is a great way to improve their musical skills and understanding.

Playing the keyboard is enormously rewarding and students will have many hours of fun ahead of them as they learn how to play.

Contents

Page	Title	New Notes	Musical Points
4	Your keyboard	**Treble clef:** Middle C	stave / treble clef
5	Broccoli And Ice Cream		♩ / ♩ / counting
6	Doughnuts And Smelly Cheese		fingering / right-hand position
7	Hedgehogs Are Awesome! Coconut Sandwiches	D	
8	Au Clair De La Lune	E	**4** time signature / 𝅝 / repeat sign :‖
9	Suo Gân Rocking		**2**
10	Elephants And Big Sardines	F	
11	Pease Pudding Hot Space Mission		
12	Merrily We Roll Along	G	ostinato
13	Happy Holiday		
14	Purple Porridge Dragons Like To Dance		♪
15	Tick, Tock, Tick, Tock		𝄾
16	Waiting For The Snowflakes		
17	Guess Which Tune...		
18	Land Ahoy!	A	**3** / ♩.
20	This Old Man		change of hand position
21	London Bridge		♩. / dotted rhythms
22	Kalinka	E♭	♭ flat sign / upbeat (anacrusis)
23	Fireworks!	low B	ties

Page	Title	New Notes	Musical Points
24	The Milky Way	B♭, C	
25	All Through The Night	F♯	♯ sharp sign
26	Max The Monster	D♯, G♯, A♯, B	2nd finger crossing thumb
27	The Scaredy-Ghost	A♭	/ thumb under 3rd finger
28	Playing with your left hand One Man Went To Mow	**Bass clef:** C, D, E, F, G	bass clef
29	Lightly Row	(A, B, Middle C)	
30	Frère Jacques	low G, A	round
31	Hot Cross Buns		/ use of right and left hand
32	Pop! Goes The Weasel	B♭	
33	Ode To Joy		dynamics / f / hands together
34	Barcarolle Suo Gân (both hands)		p
35	Strange Echoes		
36	Amazing Grace		major pentatonic scale
37	Chords/Broken Chords		chords / triads: C major, F major, G major
38	Parties Rock!		
39	Spinning Waltz		legato
40	Gliding Downwards		
41	Waiting For The Snowflakes (both hands)		
42	Isaac The Dinosaur		staccato
43	Amelia The Mouse		duet
44	The Old Steam Train		
46	Fireworks! (both hands)		left-hand chord accompaniment
47	Stomp, Stomp...Squeak!		

Your keyboard

Have a look at your keyboard. Can you see any repeated patterns?

The black keys are arranged in groups of two or three.

Your keyboard is made up of a 12-note pattern (five black keys and seven white keys) that is repeated over its entire length.

The white keys are named **A B C D E F G**.

To find note **C**, look for a group of two black keys — **C** is the note directly to the left of the two black keys.

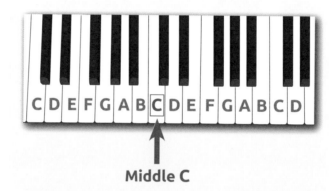

C D E F G A B C D E F G A B C D

Middle C

How many **C**s are there on your keyboard?

Now let's find **Middle C**. This should be near the middle of your keyboard — ask your teacher if you can't find it.

Sitting at your keyboard

When you play, make sure your elbows are at the same level as your hands on the keyboard, so that your forearms are **parallel** to the floor.

You may be able to adjust the height of your stool or put a cushion on your chair so that you are sitting at the best level to play.

Always try to keep your arms and hands relaxed when playing.

stave (5 horizontal lines)

Middle C

1

treble clef

Music is written on five horizontal lines called a **stave**.

A different note is written on each line and in each space on the stave.

Notes played by your right hand are usually written in the **treble clef**.

This is how you write **Middle C**. Play it now, using the thumb of your right hand.

♩ or ♩   This is a **crotchet** — it lasts one beat.

𝅗𝅥 or 𝅗𝅥   This is a **minim** — it lasts two beats.

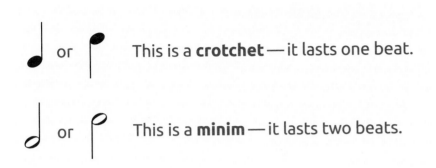

Broccoli And Ice Cream

Clap the rhythm below as you count the beats '1, 2, 3, 4...' out loud.

Then try saying the words to this rhythm.

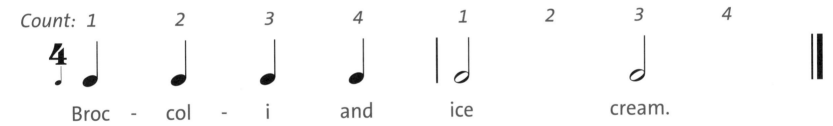

Count: 1   2   3   4   1   2   3   4

Broc – col – i and ice cream.

Now play this rhythm on the note **Middle C** using the thumb of your right hand.

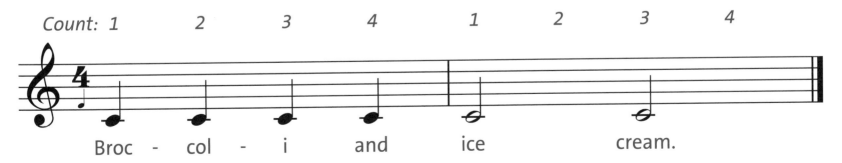

Count: 1   2   3   4   1   2   3   4

Broc – col – i and ice cream.

Doughnuts And Smelly Cheese

Clap the rhythm below as you count the beats '1, 2, 3, 4...' out loud.

Now try saying the words and clapping the rhythm at the same time.

And finally, play the rhythm on **Middle C**, counting '1, 2, 3, 4...' in your head.

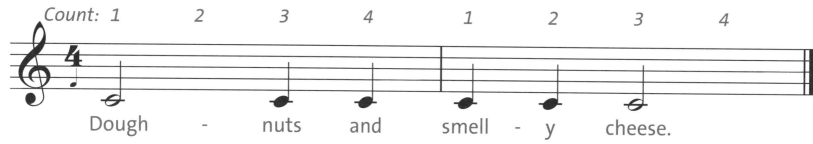

Count: 1   2   3   4   1   2   3   4

Dough – nuts and smell – y cheese.

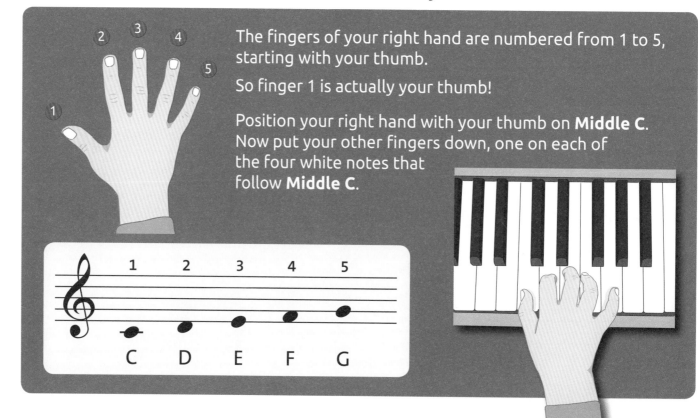

The fingers of your right hand are numbered from 1 to 5, starting with your thumb.

So finger 1 is actually your thumb!

Position your right hand with your thumb on **Middle C**. Now put your other fingers down, one on each of the four white notes that follow **Middle C**.

C D E F G

new note: D

Play D with the 2nd finger of your right hand.

These two tunes use just the notes **Middle C** and **D**.
Use the hand position opposite — you will only need to use fingers 1 and 2.

For each tune, first say the words and clap the rhythm, and then play the tune on your keyboard, counting carefully in your head.

Hedgehogs Are Awesome!

Count: 1   2   3   4   1   2   3   4

Hedge - hogs are awe - some!

Coconut Sandwiches

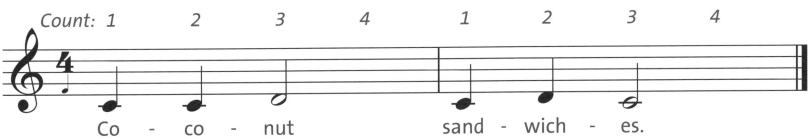

Count: 1   2   3   4   1   2   3   4

Co - co - nut sand - wich - es.

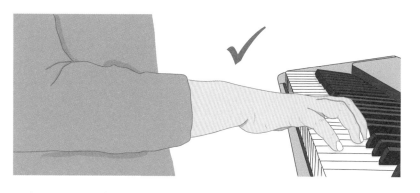

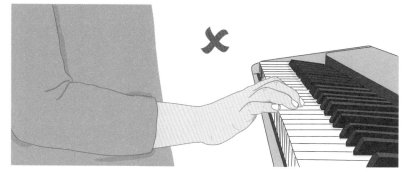

When you play, your hand should be cupped. Curve your fingers nicely and play with your fingertips, not your nails.

Don't let your wrist drop below the level of your knuckles, and remember to keep your hand and arm relaxed.

Music is divided into **bars**, each bar containing a number of beats. At the end of each bar is a **bar line**.

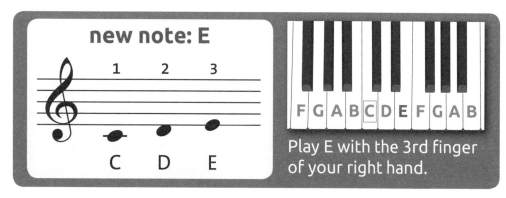

new note: E

	1	2	3
	C	D	E

F G A B C D E F G A B

Play E with the 3rd finger of your right hand.

$\mathbf{4 \atop 4}$ This is a **time signature** — it tells us there are four crotchet beats in each bar.

○ This is a **semibreve** — it lasts four beats.

𝄇 This is a **repeat sign** — it tells us to go back to the beginning and play all the music again.

Au Clair De La Lune

Say the words and clap the rhythm before you play the tune.
The fingers to play with are written above the notes.

bar lines

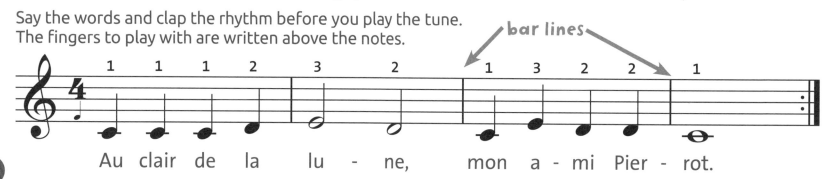

1	1	1	2	3	2	1	3	2	2	1

Au   clair   de   la   lu — ne,   mon   a - mi   Pier - rot.

Suo Gân

The fingering above the notes will help you play the tune.

This **time signature** tells us there are two crotchet beats in each bar.

Count '1 2, 1 2...' in your head as you play.

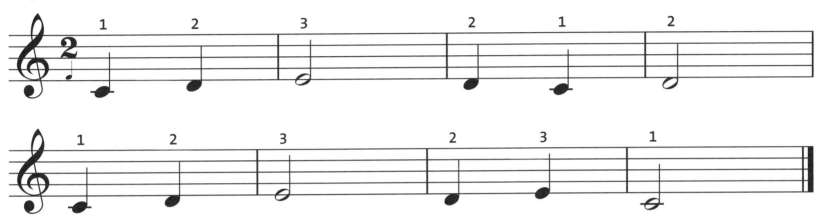

Rocking

In this tune your right hand gently rocks between notes **Middle C** and **E**, using your thumb and 3rd finger. Play the tune as smoothly as you can.

Nice and stead-y, rock-ing smooth-ly, C, E, Mid-dle C.

Try to make up your own tune using the notes **Middle C**, **D** and **E**. Begin by making up some words for your tune, and then experiment on your keyboard to find a tune that fits.

new note: F

Play F with the 4th finger of your right hand.

Elephants And Big Sardines

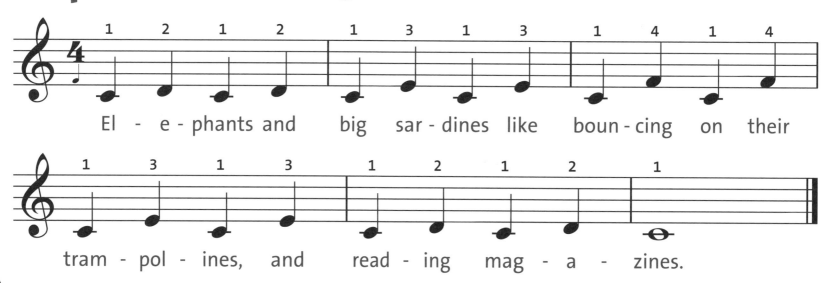

El - e - phants and big sar - dines like boun - cing on their

tram - pol - ines, and read - ing mag - a - zines.

Pease Pudding Hot

Pease pud - ding hot, pease pud - ding cold.

Pease pud-ding in the pot, nine days old!

Space Mission

Watch out for the repeat sign at the end. What does it tell you to do?

Mis - sion to the Moon, as - tro - nauts in place.

Rock - et's launch -ing soon, they're go - ing in - to out - er space.

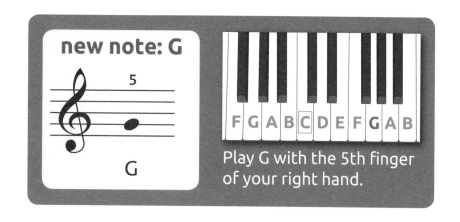

new note: G

5

G

Play G with the 5th finger of your right hand.

Class activity

Divide into two groups.

While one group plays the tune for the song below, the other group can play this bar, repeating it for the whole song:

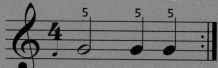

A repeating phrase like this is called an **ostinato**.

Merrily We Roll Along

Practise this song slowly to begin with while you are learning the fingering.

Mer - ri - ly we roll a - long, roll a - long, roll a - long.

Mer - ri - ly we roll a - long, o'er the dark blue sea.

Happy Holiday

Play this song steadily, making sure you don't rush.

Swim - ming in the sun, we'll have lots of fun.

Time for us to play on our hap - py hol - i - day.

Can you spot any bars that are the same in this song?

Quavers

 or

This is a **quaver** — it lasts half a beat, so there are two quavers for each crotchet count.

A pair of quavers can be joined with a beam like this:

 or

Sometimes four quavers will be joined with a beam.

Purple Porridge

Count: 1   and   2   and

Pur - ple   por - ridge.

Dragons Like To Dance

Count: 1   and   2   and   3   (4)

Drag-ons like   to dance!

This is a **crotchet rest** — it tells you to be silent for a crotchet (one beat).

Tick, Tock, Tick, Tock

Watch out for the crotchet rests in this song.

Tick,   tock,   hours on the clock.

Tock,   tick,   bet - ter be quick.   Ev - 'ry now and then   it

strikes just like Big Ben. Tick - tock, tick - tock, tick,   ding   dong!

Most of this tune is played on the notes **G** and **E** only, using fingers 5 and 3. Can you spot the single note that is different? What is the name of this note?

Waiting For The Snowflakes

Practise the first bar on its own until you are comfortable playing this phrase.

How many times does this musical phrase happen in the song? Look carefully — the phrase always begins on the second beat of the bar, but there isn't always a crotchet rest on the first beat!

I'm wait - ing for the snow - flakes, they will dust the

fro - zen ground, I'm so ex - ci - ted. Can't wait for those flakes

ma - king pret - ty shapes, I'm wait-ing for the snow.

Guess Which Tune...

Practise these five musical phrases with a friend or your teacher.

Then, take it in turns to pick a tune to play, and let the other person try to work out which one is being played. Listen carefully for the shape of the melody and its rhythm.

The note names of one of these musical phrases spells out a word. Can you spot which one it is?

Land Ahoy!

Use the new right-hand position shown opposite to play this song. The time signature tells us there are three crotchet beats in each bar, so count '1, 2, 3...' in your head as you play.

Before you play, say the words and clap along until you are confident with the rhythm.

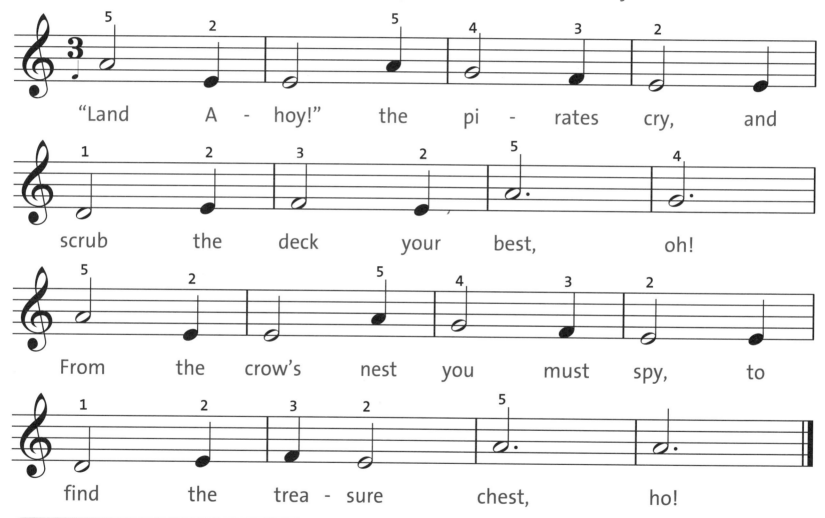

Experiment with the different sounds on your keyboard and choose one that you think works well for this jaunty pirate song.

Playing Land Ahoy!

new note: A

5

A

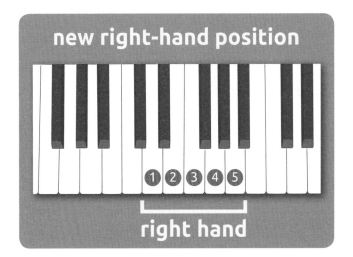

new right-hand position

right hand

New time signature

3

This **time signature** tells us there are three crotchet beats in each bar.

This is a **dotted minim** — it lasts three beats.

A dot after a note tells you to lengthen the note by half of its normal value.

♩. = ♩ + ♪

3 = 2 + 1

This Old Man

Begin by putting your right hand in the position shown on page 19, with your thumb on D.

Your hand will change position on the second beat of bar 4, marked with an arrow — use finger 3 here, as shown in the fingering, and your hand will then be in a new position that will take you through to the end of the song.

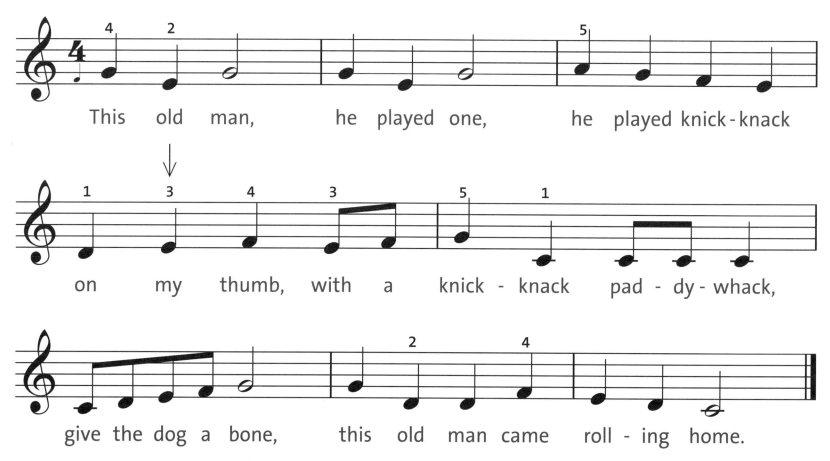

You could try playing **Amelia The Mouse** on page 43 now. It uses all the notes you have learnt so far and includes some changes of hand position and some stretches.

This is a **dotted crotchet** — it lasts one-and-a-half beats:

♩. = ♩ + ♪

1½ = 1 + ½

Repeat the first bar of **London Bridge** a few times to practise the dotted rhythm, counting carefully in your head.

To make sure you play the quaver at the right time after the dotted crotchet, count in quavers: '1 and 2 and 3 and 4 and...'

Count: 1 (and) (2) and

Lon - don

London Bridge

Position your right hand as shown on page 19 before you begin, but watch for the change of hand position near the end, shown by the arrow.

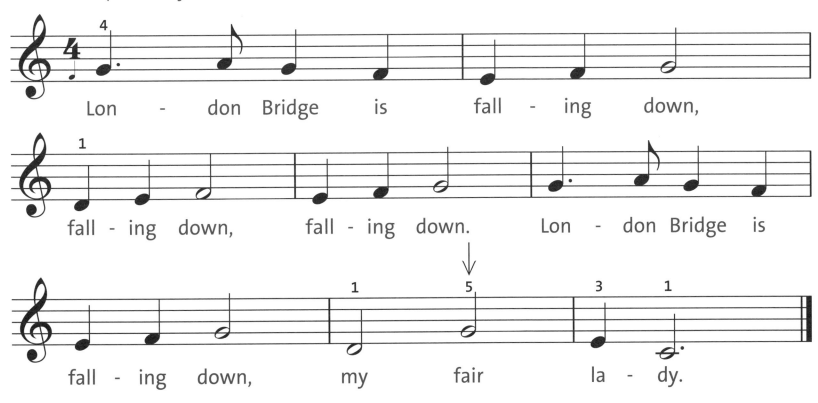

Lon - don Bridge is fall - ing down, fall - ing down, fall - ing down. Lon - don Bridge is fall - ing down, my fair la - dy.

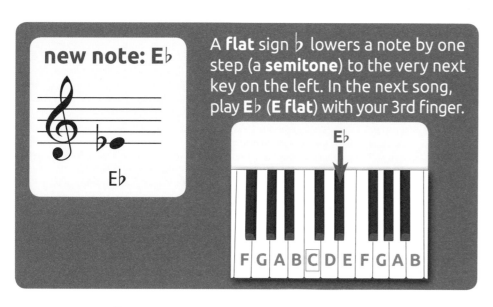

Kalinka

This song begins on the second beat of the bar. A note at the beginning of a tune that comes before the first full bar is called an **upbeat** (or **anacrusis**). The extra beat at the start is taken off the last bar, to balance.

Practise this tune with a steady beat to begin with. When you are confident, begin slowly and get gradually faster and faster as you play through.

You could try starting quietly and getting gradually louder through your performance as well.

new note: B

B

A **tie** is a curved line that joins two notes of the same pitch.

Only the first note is played and held for the length of both **tied** notes.

Fireworks

Your hand position shifts a number of times in this song. It begins with the first position you learnt on page 6, but the first shift comes very soon afterwards when you play the note B with your thumb (finger 1).

Count carefully and remember not to play during the crotchet rests.

Gold and sil - ver flare_____

shoot - ing in the air._____ The rock - ets, foun - tains too, are

red and green and blue;_____ I can't help but stare._____

new notes: B♭ and C

B♭   C

C D E F G A B C D

new right-hand position

Place the thumb of your right hand on the **F** above **Middle C**. Now put your other fingers down, on the notes **G**, **A**, **B♭** (**B flat**) and **C**, as shown.

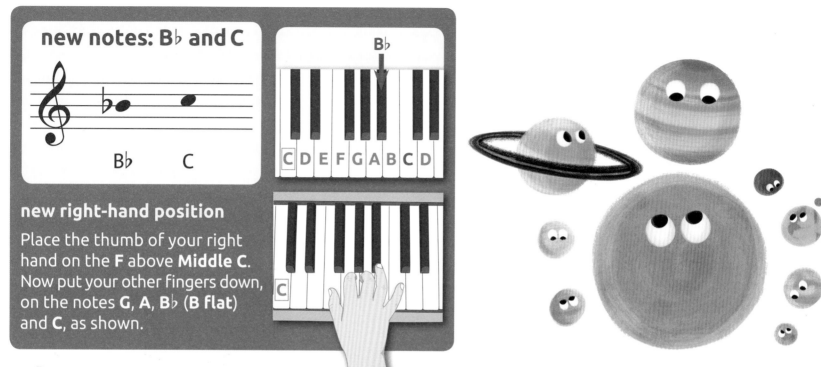

The Milky Way

Watch out for the ties in this song. Practise this rhythm with finger 2 on the note G a few times before you play:

Count: 1   2   and   (3)

Ju - pi -ter___ and   Mer -cur -y___ and   ma -ny stars too   far   to see.___

So much more__ in our   gal - a -xy___ that's called the Milk - y   Way.

24

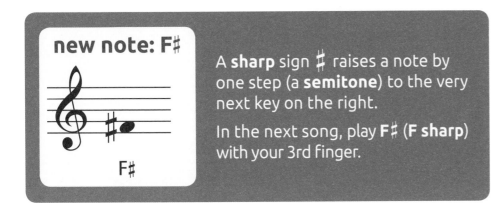

new note: F#

F#

A **sharp** sign ♯ raises a note by one step (a **semitone**) to the very next key on the right.

In the next song, play **F♯** (**F sharp**) with your 3rd finger.

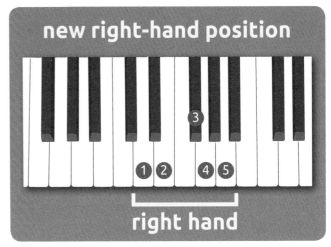

new right-hand position

right hand

All Through The Night

Remember practising your dotted rhythm for **London Bridge** on page 21? Count carefully in your head to make sure the quavers that follow the dotted crotchets in this song are played at the right time.

Have a look at the first four-bar phrase of this tune, and then the second four-bar phrase. What do you notice?

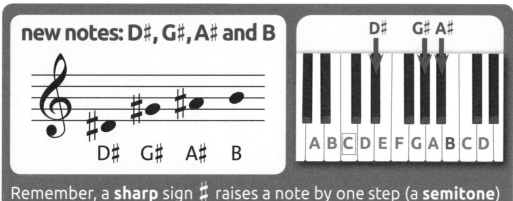

new notes: D♯, G♯, A♯ and B

D♯   G♯   A♯   B

D♯   G♯ A♯

A B C D E F G A B C D

Remember, a **sharp** sign ♯ raises a note by one step (a **semitone**) to the very next key on the right.

Look at these new notes — **D♯** is another name for **E♭**, and **A♯** is another name for **B♭**.

Max The Monster

Watch out for where your 2nd finger crosses over your thumb on the bottom line of music.
For fun, you could make a "Grrrrrrr!" sound with your voice on the last note.

Max   The   Mon - ster   mis - be - haved,   his

moth - er   sent   him   to   his   cave.   Go

in   if   you   feel   brave!   Grrrrrrr!

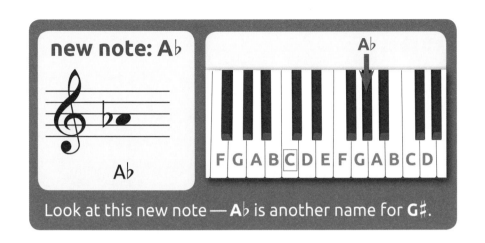

new note: A♭

A♭

Look at this new note — **A♭** is another name for **G♯**.

This is a **minim rest** — it tells you to be silent for a minim (two beats).

The Scaredy-Ghost

Watch the fingering carefully, especially where your thumb goes under your 3rd finger.

The ghost in the cas - tle's go - ing "Woo - oo".

She's cold and her lone - li - ness won't end.

I guess she is just as scared as you - hoo,

so may - be you - hoo should try to be her friend. Woo - hoo!

Playing with your left hand

The fingers of your left hand are numbered from 1 to 5, starting with your thumb.

Find the **C** below **Middle C** and place your little finger (finger 5) on it.

Now put your other fingers down, one on each of the four white notes that follow **C**.

One Man Went To Mow

Use the hand position above to play this song. Notice that notes for your left hand are written in a different clef—it is called the **bass clef** (see opposite).

One man went to mow, went to mow a mea-dow.

One man and his dog... woof!... went to mow a mea-dow.

Lightly Row

This song is also played by your left hand and uses the hand position shown opposite.

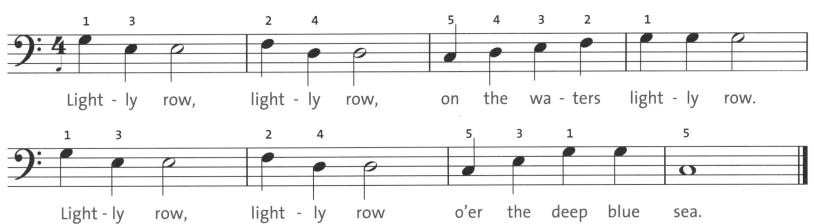

Light - ly row, light - ly row, on the wa - ters light - ly row.

Light - ly row, light - ly row o'er the deep blue sea.

Left-hand notes

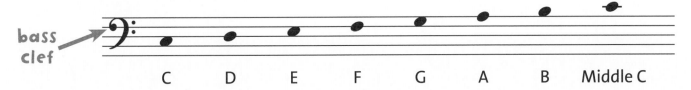

bass clef

C   D   E   F   G   A   B   Middle C

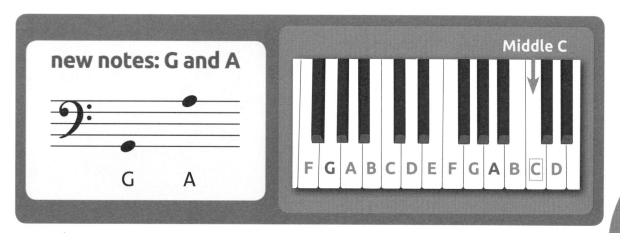

new notes: G and A

G A

Middle C

F G A B C D E F G A B C D

Class activity

Divide into two groups and try this as a **round**.

One group begins, and when they reach bar 3, the second group begins. Each group plays the tune through twice.

Frère Jacques

In bars 5 and 6, your 2nd finger reaches over your thumb and back again (at the points marked ✳). Practise these bars on their own a few times to master this. Also, watch out for the change of hand position near the end.

Frè - re Jac - ques, Frè - re Jac - ques,

dor - mez vous? Dor - mez vous? Son - nez les mat - i - nes!

Son - nez les mat - i - nes! Ding, dang, dong! Ding, dang, dong!

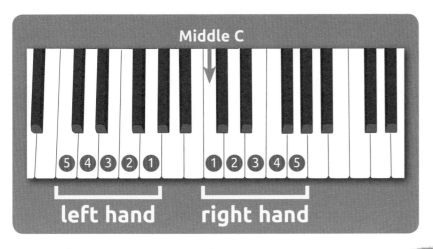

This is a **semibreve rest** — it tells you to be silent for a semibreve (four beats).

It can also be used to show a full bar's rest in any time signature.

Hot Cross Buns

You're going to need both hands for this song! Get them in the positions shown above before you begin to play.

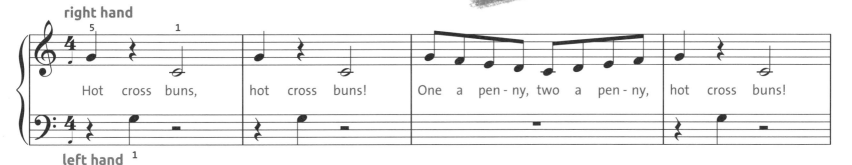

Pop! Goes The Weasel

Before you play, look at the fingering on the first note in both hands to find out where to position them.

In this song, the 2nd finger of your left hand is used to play B♭.

As in **Hot Cross Buns**, the tune passes between your hands.

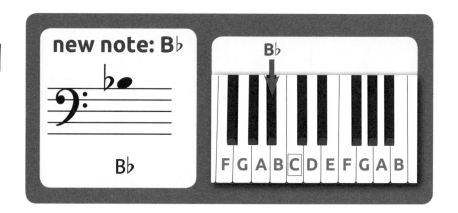

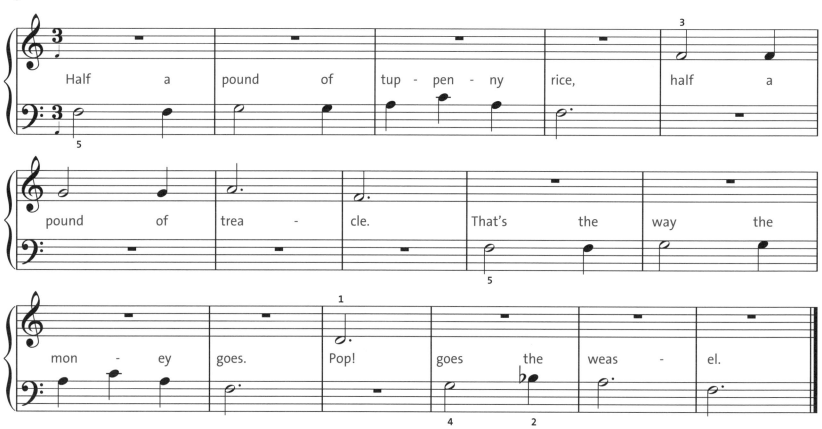

Ode To Joy

by Ludwig van Beethoven

Watch out for the **tie** (in both hands) between bars 12 and 13 on the bottom line of music.

Dynamics

Dynamic marks tell you how loudly or quietly to play.

f   This sign stands for **forte** (pronounced 'for-tay'), meaning loud.

This piece starts in your left hand then moves to your right hand, and by the end, you are playing with both hands together. Well done!

p This dynamic marks stands for **piano** (pronounced 'pea-ah-no'), meaning quiet.

Class activity

For the next two songs, divide into two groups.

While one group plays the right hand, the other can play the left-hand part.

Barcarolle by Jacques Offenbach

Your hands move together in **parallel** in this piece. Practise your right hand on its own first, and then your left hand. Finally, put them together.

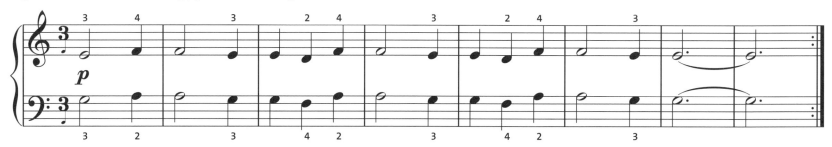

Suo Gân

Do you remember this melody from page 9? Your right hand is the same here, but now it is accompanied by your left hand, which moves in parallel.

Practise them hands separately to begin with before putting them together.

Strange Echoes

Use the same positions for your right and left hands that you used for **Hot Cross Buns** on page 31.

Try to make the echoes with words in brackets quieter than the rest of the tune.

Can you spot any other phrases in the music that are like echoes?

Can you hear the faint-est ech - o?___ (Ech - o)___ It's a most un - u - sual

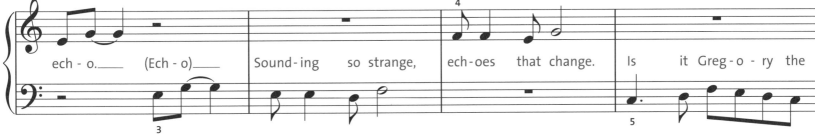

ech - o.___ (Ech - o)___ Sound-ing so strange, ech-oes that change. Is it Greg-o-ry the

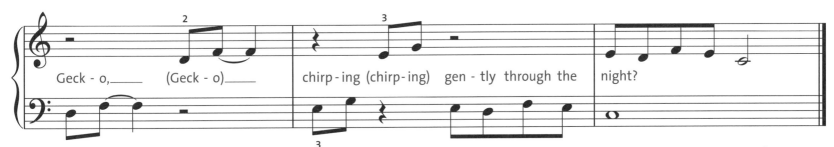

Geck - o,___ (Geck - o)___ chirp-ing (chirp-ing) gen-tly through the night?

Amazing Grace

Your left hand is in a fixed position for this song (the same position as used on page 32), but your right hand moves around quite a lot. Following the right-hand fingering will make it easier to play.

This song uses only five different notes in its melody. These notes form the **major pentatonic scale**.

Can you make up a tune using only these notes? Your teacher could accompany you (using the chords F, Dm and B♭).

F G A C D

Chords

When three or more notes are played together they make a **chord**. Chords can be used to accompany tunes.

The chords below are called **triads** as they each have three notes. They are the chords of **C major**, **F major** and **G major**. Each chord is shown by a **chord symbol** written in bold above the stave (**C**, **F** and **G**).

Try playing each of these chords in your right hand — the names of the notes are written next to the stave to help you find each chord.

Now try playing them with your left hand.

Broken chords

Sometimes **broken chords** are used as an accompaniment. Instead of playing the notes of a chord at the same time, you play a broken chord by playing the notes of a chord one after the other.

This piece, for the right hand, includes broken chords.

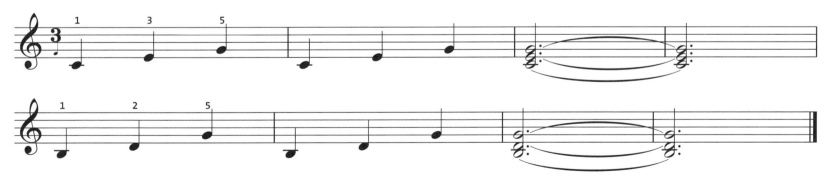

Can you work out the name of the chords that are played as broken chords in the piece above?

Parties Rock!

Practise your right-hand chords on their own to begin with, before adding your left hand. For each chord, make sure you play all three notes at exactly the same time.

Here are the first two bars of the right-hand chords written with a different rhythm. Try to play the whole piece again using this rhythm in each bar for your right-hand chords.

Can you make up your own rhythm to play your right-hand chords to?

Spinning Waltz

A **waltz** is a type of dance with three beats in each bar.

Try to play the broken chords in your right hand smoothly, making the notes connected — this style of playing is called **legato**.

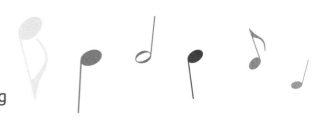

Left-hand notes reminder

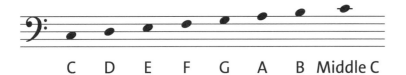

C   D   E   F   G   A   B   Middle C

Gliding Downwards

This song is for your left hand only. Play it smoothly, in a **legato** style.

Watch out for the bars where you play two notes at the same time.

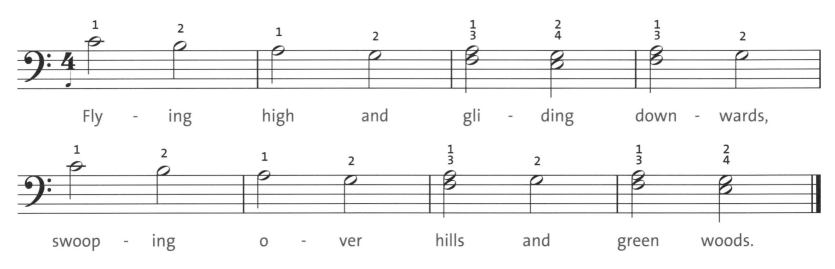

Fly - ing   high   and   gli - ding   down - wards,

swoop - ing   o - ver   hills   and   green   woods.

Experiment with the different sounds on your keyboard and choose one that you think works well for a song about a kite gliding and swooping around.

Waiting For The Snowflakes

Do you remember this right-hand melody from page 16? Here, it is accompanied by the left hand you have just learnt in **Gliding Downwards**. Practise each hand separately before putting them together.

I'm wait - ing for the snow - flakes, they will dust the fro - zen ground, I'm so ex - ci - ted. Can't wait for those flakes ma - king pret - ty shapes, I'm wait - ing for the snow.

If your keyboard has a record function, you could record the left hand on its own and then play it back, playing along with the right hand. You might also want to perform this song as a duet.

Duet Time!

A dot above or below a note tells you to make the note shorter than its written length.

These are called **staccato** notes.

Play them lightly and with a bounce — imagine you have touched something hot!

Isaac The Dinosaur

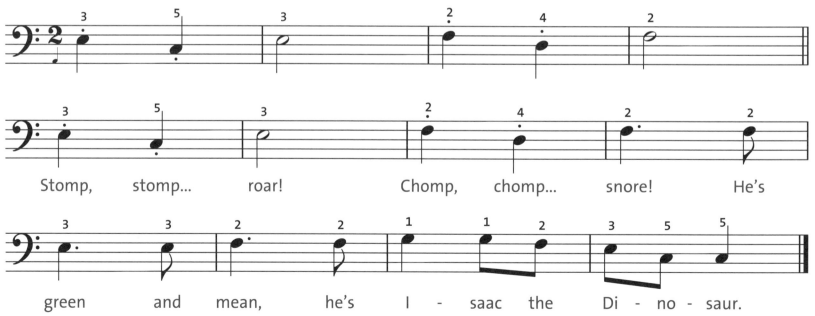

Stomp, stomp... roar! Chomp, chomp... snore! He's green and mean, he's I - saac the Di - no - saur.

Amelia The Mouse

Count carefully through the bars of rests in the introduction.

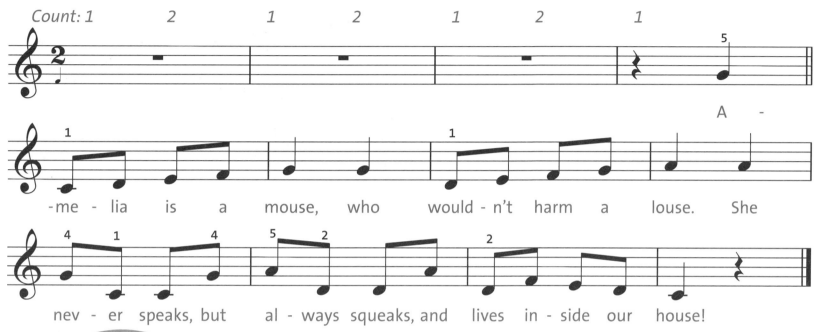

-me - lia   is   a   mouse,   who   would - n't   harm   a   louse.   She

nev - er   speaks, but   al - ways   squeaks, and   lives   in - side   our   house!

Class activity

Divide into two groups. One group can play **Amelia The Mouse** while the other group plays **Isaac The Dinosaur** as an accompaniment— the tunes fit together.

Try playing this song with short **staccato** notes, as if dots had been written underneath each note.

You'll find these two songs combined on page 47, as a solo piece.

The Old Steam Train

This song has a repeating left-hand accompaniment.

Do you remember what a repeating musical phrase like this is called? Have a look at page 12.

This left-hand figure repeats all the way through to the last two bars, marked *.

Chug - ging down the track,

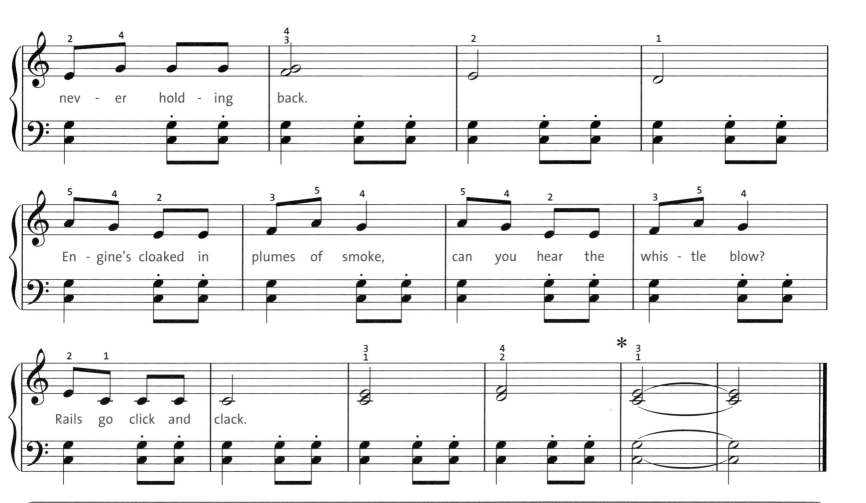

Lyrics under the staff:
nev - er hold - ing back.

En - gine's cloaked in plumes of smoke, can you hear the whis - tle blow?

Rails go click and clack.

Class activity   You can play this as an ensemble piece in up to three parts.

Divide into three groups. Group 1 will play the right-hand part and Group 2 will play the left-hand part. Group 3 (optional) can play the two-bar ostinato below (figure **I**), repeating it until they reach the last two bars (marked ✳), when they play figure **II**.

Fireworks!

Do you remember this song? You learnt the right-hand part on page 23.

Your left hand repeats this sequence of chords until the last two bars.

Keep your left-hand chords quieter than your right hand so that the tune can sing out over the accompaniment. You might also want to perform this song as a duet.

Gold and sil - ver flare___ shoot - ing in the air.___

___ The rock - ets, foun - tains too, are

red and green and blue;___ I can't help but stare.___

Stomp, Stomp...Squeak!

This song partners two songs you've already learnt hands separately—**Amelia The Mouse** in your right hand and **Isaac The Dinosaur** in your left hand. You can now play them hands together.